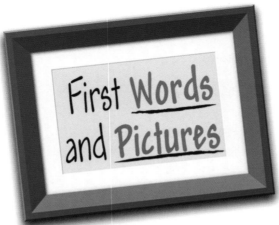

First Words
and Pictures

My
Busy Day

By Ruth Owen, Emma Randall, and Sophie Murphy

Ruby Tuesday Books

Published in 2017 by Ruby Tuesday Books Ltd.

Copyright © 2017 Ruby Tuesday Books Ltd.

Editor: Mark J. Sachner
Production: John Lingham

Photo Credits:
Photographs courtesy of Shutterstock

Library of Congress Control Number: 2017908518

Print ISBN: 978-1-911341-83-3
eBook ISBN: 978-1-911341-84-0

Printed and published in the United States of America

For further information including rights and permissions requests, please contact our Customer Service Department at 877-377-8577.

What's Inside the Book?

yawn

clock

It's Morning!

toothpaste

toothbrush

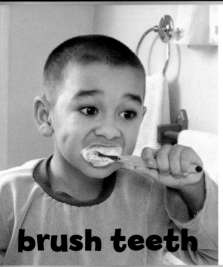
brush teeth

brush hair

toilet

flush

toilet paper

wash hands

soap

towel

potty

diaper

5

shirt

buttons

sweater

Time to Get Dressed

belt

jeans

zipper

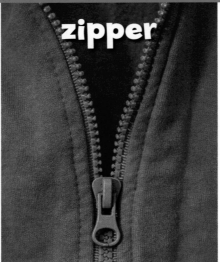

hoodie

undershirt

panties

dress

T-shirt

underpants

shorts

turtleneck

skirt

pants

Can you find the matching pair of socks?

7

eat

drink

Time for Breakfast

cereal

bowl

oatmeal

8

scrambled eggs

toast

sticky

jam

toaster

spread

peanut butter

pour

bagel

cup

orange juice

cream cheese

9

tie laces

boots

shoe

Off to School

car

car seat

seat belt

coat

scarf

hat

bus

scooter

walk

bike

crosswalk

11

school

classroom

Welcome to Our School

friends

teacher

pencil

a b c d e f g h i j k l m n o p q r s t u v w x y z

alphabet

book

numbers

table

chair

reading

painting

writing

13

gardening

sand

Things We Do

puzzle

Duck

play area

14

guitar

bongos

xylophone

drum

maracas

making music

tambourine

15

wash hands

lunch

Time for Lunch

water

yogurt

tuna

cheese

carrot sticks

baked potato

peas

sandwich

fruit

mashed potato

fish sticks

cucumber

omelet

MILK
ONE PINT (473mL)

milk

17

sharing

hugging

Things We Do and Feel

raising
hands

helping

laughing

crying

happy

How do you feel today?

sad

shy

excited

19

running

dancing

On the Move!

kick

soccer ball

yoga

swimming

water wings

swimsuit

trunks

paddle

ball

hoops

What is your favorite sport or game?

throw

catch

21

library

supermarket

Places We Go

playground

park

duck
pond

22

doctor

dentist

assistant

birthday party

vet

kitten

washing machine

cooking

Around My Home

dishwasher

lawn mower

couch

tablet

screen

laptop

keyboard

phone

vacuum cleaner

television

remote

25

wash hands

family

Time for Dinner

spaghetti

stir-fry

tacos

rice

beans

grapes

fish

knife

plate

fork

salad

chicken

pizza

sausages

broccoli

corn

27

sleepy

bath

Time for Bed

brush teeth

bedtime story

slippers

bunk beds

pajamas

teddy bear

pillow

kiss

quilt

goodnight

29

Tips and Ideas

Look ✓ Read ✓ Talk ✓ Discover ✓ Learn ✓

This book is designed to help you and your child get the best learning experience possible. We suggest that you make yourselves comfortable within a quiet environment and allow your child to hold the book and turn the pages. When you and your child are reading the book, pause to allow your child to *read* a word or ask questions about the pictures and words.

Page 5: After your child has used the toilet or potty, allow him or her to pull up their underpants. Then ask your child what they need to do next. If your child does not know, remind him or her that it's important to wash their hands to keep germs from spreading.
1) Wet hands with clean water.
2) Apply soap.
3) Rub and scrub for 20 seconds.
4) Rinse with clean water.
5) Dry with a towel.

Pages 8-9: Give your child some fruit cut into small pieces. Ask the child to make a face from the different fruit shapes. When the face is complete, eat it all up!

Pages 10-11: Ask your child how he or she got to day care or preschool today, and discuss the journey. You can use toy cars or buses as props during your chat. Point out the pictures of the car seat and crosswalk. Talk about keeping safe—for example, why should a child sit in a car seat, or why do drivers stop at traffic lights? If the child walked to school, discuss the importance of crossing guards at intersections and crosswalks.

Pages 6-7: Ask your child what items of clothing he or she is wearing today. Do the clothes have buttons or a zipper?

Pages 16-17: Ask your child to point to or say their favorite foods on these pages, and on pages 8–9 and 26–27. Ask them what other foods they like to eat. Discuss with your child the importance of making the right food choices. Download a free healthy-eating chart and a fun activity about making food choices from:

www.rubytuesdaybooks.com/firstwords

Page 25: Find an old phone or laptop and remove the battery. Allow the child to use this technology to mimic what he or she sees in everyday life. You can use your own phone to join in with the role-playing.
Ask questions such as:
• Who are you talking to on the phone?
• What are you doing on the laptop?
• What happens when you tap on the keyboard?

Pages 18-19: Discuss what is happening in the pictures with your child. Ask questions such as:
• How do you think the girls who are hugging feel?
• How do you think the girl who fell over feels now that her friend has helped her?
• What do you think could have made the boy cry? Do you think that a hug might make him feel better?

Pages 28-29: Look at the pictures and ask your child about their bedtime routine.
• Do you have a favorite bath-time toy? What is it?
• Do you share a bedroom with anyone?
• What do you wear to bed?
• Who reads you a bedtime story?
• Do you have a teddy bear or a special blanket?

Busy Day Activities

Make a Feelings Chart

Go online to find photos that show different facial expressions—for example, happy, sad, scared, shy, sick. Print, cut out, and write the feelings word beneath the face. (You can also draw faces.) Stick adhesive putty to the back of each face. Take a piece of cardstock and write "**How am I feeling today?**" at the top. Pin the cardstock to a wall or stick it to the refrigerator.

Ask your child how he or she is feeling at different times of the day. The child can say or point to the relevant face, and then stick the face beneath the question.

Let's Make Music!

Create your own musical instruments with your child. Make a drum out of a saucepan and hit it with a wooden spoon. Create a shaker with a plastic bottle that's half-filled with uncooked rice or pasta.

Go on a "Places in Our Community" Hunt

Create a checklist with photographs of different places in your local community—for example, a school, church, mosque, park, supermarket, crosswalk, doctor's office, fire station, restaurant, or gas station.

When you're out and about, encourage your child to say when they spot the place. Check off the place on the list and then discuss with your child what happens in that building or community area.

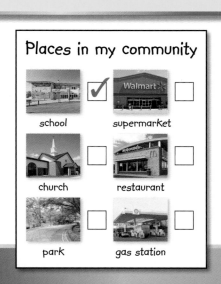